Inspir

SAFETY INVENTIONS
Inspired by Nature

by Lisa J. Amstutz

PEBBLE
a capstone imprint

First Facts is published by Pebble,
1710 Roe Crest Drive, North Mankato, Minnesota 56003
www.capstonepub.com

Library of Congress Cataloging-in-Publication Data
Names: Amstutz, Lisa J., author.
Title: Safety inventions inspired by nature / by Lisa Amstutz.
Description: North Mankato, MN : Pebble, a Capstone imprint, [2020] |
Series: First facts. Inspired by nature | Audience: Ages 6-9. | Audience:
K to grade 3. | Includes bibliographical references and index.
Identifiers: LCCN 2019006441 | ISBN 9781977108388 (library binding) |
ISBN 9781977110084 (pbk.) | ISBN 9781977108579 (ebook pdf)
Subjects: LCSH: Inventions—Juvenile literature. | Biomimicry—Juvenile
literature. | Industrial safety—Juvenile literature.
Classification: LCC T15 .A5845 2019 | DDC 609--dc23
LC record available at https://lccn.loc.gov/2019006441

Editorial Credits
Abby Colich and Jaclyn Jaycox, editors; Juliette Peters, designer;
Jo Miller, media researcher; Katy LaVigne, production specialist

Photo Credits
b=bottom, l=left, m=middle, r=right, t=top
Alamy: Tribune Content Agency LLC, 17b; AP Images: Keith Srakocic, Cover,
7r; Newscom: Gus Regalado/Album, 21t; Science Source: Claus Lunau,
11t, Pascal Goetgheluck, 13br, Raul Gonzalez, 13bl, USDA/Peggy Greb, 5;
Shutterstock: BalkansCat, 1l, 9, Christian Vinces, 11b, hxdbzxy, 7l, Kenny
CMK, 19t, metamorworks, 15b, NaniP, 1m, 15t, Rawpixel.com, 19b, sahua d,
21b, Sten Roosvald, 1r, 17t, Yann hubert, 13t

Design Elements
Shutterstock: Zubada

Printed and bound in China.
001671

Table of Contents

Ideas from Nature

Nature is full of good ideas. Some scientists study nature. They use what they learn to make new things. Copying ideas from nature is called biomimicry. Ideas from nature can help keep people safe.

Scientists study nature to help solve human problems.

Search Like a Snake

Earthquakes and tornadoes damage buildings. People can become trapped inside. Rescue workers must find them quickly. It's a dangerous job. A "snake" robot can help. It moves like a real snake. It can squirm through **rubble**. Lights and cameras on the robot help the rescue workers see inside.

Fact
Scientists are copying a snake's skin too. They studied how a snake can slither over objects so easily. Some machines may one day move more like snakes.

rubble—broken bricks, concrete, glass, metal, and other debris left from a building that has fallen down

Watch Your Head!

A woodpecker pounds its beak on wood all day. But it doesn't hurt its head. Soft **cartilage** keeps its brain safe. One inventor used this idea. He made a safer bike helmet. It has special cardboard inside. It protects the rider's head.

cartilage—a strong, rubbery tissue that connects bones in people and animals

inspire—to influence and encourage someone to do something

Fact

Other animals have also **inspired** new helmets. Scientists have made helmets using ideas from a turtle's shell and a hedgehog's quills.

Catching the Waves

Dolphins use sound waves to find food. These waves move easily through water. Scientists have made **sensors** that can find sound waves underwater. They can pick up the sound waves from underwater earthquakes. Scientists use these sound waves to study **tsunamis**. Soon they may be able to warn people when a big wave is near.

---

echolocation—the process of using sounds and echoes to locate objects; whales and dolphins use echolocation to find food

sensor—an instrument that detects changes and sends information to a controlling device

tsunami—a series of ocean waves caused by an underwater earthquake or volcano

Fact

The process that dolphins use to find food is called **echolocation**. Whales and bats use echolocation too.

Dolphins send out sound waves to find prey. The waves bounce off the prey and back to the dolphin.

Ants to the Rescue

When ants face danger, they send out a signal. More ants come to help. They attack as a **swarm**. Computer scientists used this idea. They made digital "ants." This "swarm" moves through a computer. The ants look for malware. Malware programs steal information and harm computers. Digital ants protect computers and keep information safe.

swarm—a large number of bugs together in a group

Saving Water

Another bug may help out humans. The Namib Desert beetle lives in dry places. Tiny bumps on its back collect water from fog. The beetle tilts forward. It drinks the water that runs down. A new device uses this idea. It collects water from fog. It may soon provide clean water in dry areas.

swarm of ants

Fighting Germs

A shark's skin is made of tiny toothlike plates. These plates keep **algae** and **fungi** from growing. Scientists have made a material that's like shark skin. It is used for hospital equipment. It keeps germs from growing. This material helps protect people from disease.

algae—plantlike organisms that live mostly in water

fungi—a type of organism that has no leaves, flowers, or roots

resistant—able to fight off or withstand something

Fact

Over time, some germs can become **resistant** to drugs. They can cause diseases that are difficult to treat. Shark skin material can help stop these germs from spreading.

shark scales

shark skin material

15

A Bug's Eye View

Locusts fly in large swarms. But they rarely bump into one another. They focus on the insects right in front of them. Scientists used this idea. They are working on making sensors for self-driving cars. The sensors will detect objects around them. They will help keep the cars from crashing.

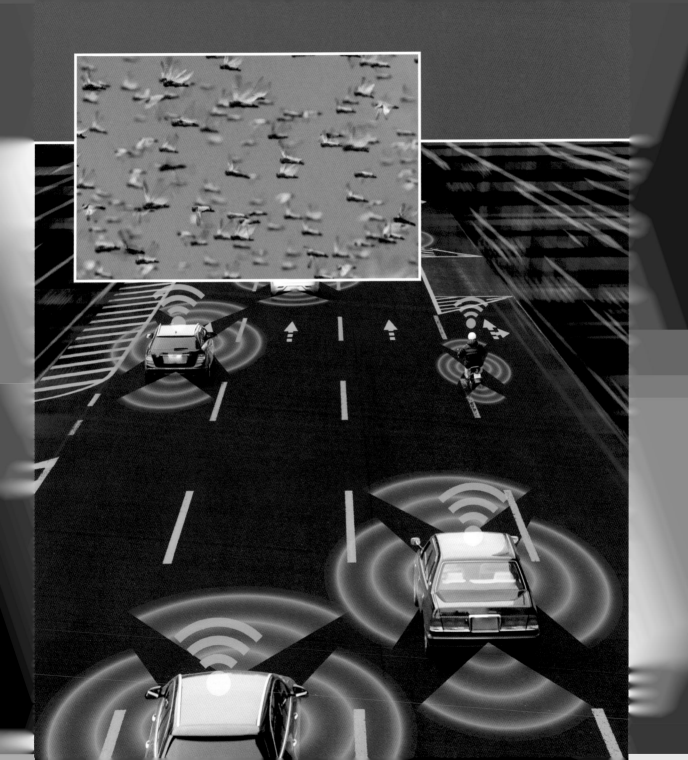

Spiderweb Glass

Thump! Birds crash into windows every day. But thanks to spiders, birds may be safer! Spiderwebs reflect **ultraviolet (UV) light**. Birds can see this reflection. Scientists created a new glass. It reflects UV light the same way spiderwebs do. To people, the glass looks clear. But birds know to stay away.

---

ultraviolet light—rays of light that cannot be seen by the human eye

Fact
Humans cannot see UV light, but many animals can.

From Bats to Scanners

Bats fly and hunt in the dark night. They send out sound waves. They listen for the echoes that bounce back. The echoes help them find food. Airport scanners use the same idea. They send out sound waves. The echoes form an image on a screen. They help workers spot weapons. They keep travelers safe.

toxin—a poisonous substance made by a living thing

Turkey Detectors

Bats aren't the only winged animal inspiring safety. The skin on a turkey's head changes color with its mood. Scientists studied how the skin does this. They made an air sensor that works the same way. It can find **toxins** in the air.

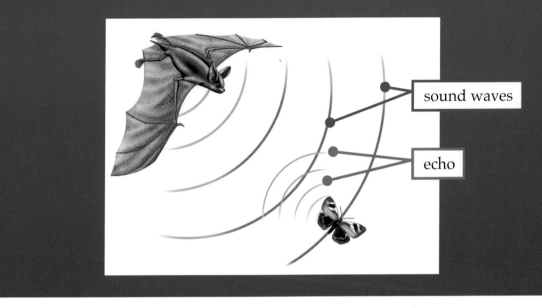

sound waves

echo

FULL-BODY SCANNER

② The body is scanned.

PLEASE
raise your arms
according to picture.

① Person is asked to raise
his or her arms.

③ A scanned image appears
on a computer screen.

Glossary

algae (AL-jee)—plantlike organisms that live mostly in water

cartilage (KAHR-tuh-lij)—a strong, rubbery tissue that connects bones in people and animals

echolocation (eh-koh-loh-KAY-shuhn)—the process of using sounds and echoes to locate objects; whales and dolphins use echolocation to find food

fungi (FUHN-jy)—organisms that have no leaves, flowers, or roots

inspire (in-SPIRE)—to fill someone with an emotion, an idea, or an attitude

resistant (ree-ZISS-tent)—able to fight off or withstand something

rubble (RUHB-uhl)—broken bricks, concrete, glass, metal, and other debris left from a building that has fallen down

sensor (SEN-sur)—an instrument that detects changes and sends information to a controlling device

swarm (SWARM)—a large number of bugs together in a group

toxin (TOK-sin)—a poisonous substance made by a living thing

tsunami (tsoo-NAH-mee)—a series of ocean waves caused by an underwater earthquake or volcano

ultraviolet light (uhl-truh-VYE-uh-lit LITE)—rays of light that cannot be seen by the human eye

Read More

Bell, Samantha S. *Everyday Inventions Inspired by Nature*. Technology Inspired by Nature. Mendota Heights, MN: Focus Readers, 2018.

Colby, Jennifer. *Cat's Eyes to Reflectors*. Tech from Nature. North Mankato, MN: Cherry Lake, 2019.

Martin, Brett S. *Search-and-Rescue Robots*. Robot Innovations. North Mankato, MN: Abdo, 2018.

Internet Sites

Everyday Mysteries: Biomimicry for Kids
https://www.loc.gov/rr/scitech/mysteries/biomimicry.html

How We Make Stuff
https://www.made2bmadeagain.org/creatures_cwdtd

Kids Konnect: Inventors and Inventions
https://kidskonnect.com/history/inventors-inventions/

Critical Thinking Questions

1. How does a "snake" robot help rescue workers?

2. Echolocation has inspired scientists to make underwater sensors. What is echolocation?

3. Can you think of another use for the shark skin material discussed on page 14? Explain why you think it would be helpful.

Index